Shipwreck
in the
South China Sea

Claire Daniel

Contents

Rigby
A Harcourt Achieve Imprint

www.Rigby.com
1-800-531-5015

1 A Terrible Accident

It was a quiet winter's night on February 5, 1822.
The sky over the ocean had been black for several hours.
The nearly 2,000 people aboard the Chinese **junk** *Tek Sing*
(True Star) expected to complete their journey soon.

On deck about 1,600 men, women, and children rested. Some were probably thinking about the new life they would soon have. Unable to find jobs in China, most were **emigrating**—moving from one country to another—to the island of Java to find work.

Sailors who weren't working played games to pass the time. Another ship, the *Capella Mera,* sailed nearby. The wind was good, so both boats sailed swiftly and smoothly. No one saw the danger ahead.

What Is a Chinese Junk?

A Chinese junk is a ship that carries people and goods over the ocean or sea. In the 19th century, if the junk was from Amoy, like the *Tek Sing,* the front of the junk was painted green. If it was from Canton, the junk's front was red.

Suddenly the *Tek Sing* crashed into a group of rocks hidden below the water. As the boat turned over on its side, people spilled into the dark ocean. To help keep themselves from drowning, they wildly grabbed umbrellas and bamboo canes that had fallen off the sides of the boat. The waves threw the giant boat back and forth against the underwater rocks, ripping giant holes in the ship's sides.

Some of the people thrown overboard had to hang onto bundles of bamboo or rattan poles. Bamboo has a hollow center, which helps it float.

Some people were tossed around in the water. Others clutched onto parts of the ship. They cried to the people aboard the *Capella Mera* for help, but only 18 people were picked up before the *Capella Mera* sailed away. The sailors on the *Capella Mera* were afraid their ship would become overloaded and sink, too, if they took any more people aboard.

An hour after the crash, the *Tek Sing* turned back upright . . . and then sank slowly into the sea, never to rise again.

2 Leaving Amoy

A few weeks earlier, on January 14, 1822, the Chinese city of Amoy had been filled with excitement as the *Tek Sing* prepared for its journey. Many people were in the city to see the Chinese junk *Tek Sing* leave the harbor.

Mast a long pole that holds up a ship's sails

Stern the back part of the ship, where a sailor steers the junk

Rudder a flat piece of wood that steers the ship right or left

Heavy, wooden anchors held the *Tek Sing* floating in one place. Smaller loading boats *(sampans)* brought goods from shore to the huge junk to be loaded aboard. The junk could hold a large amount of goods, and the crew packed each of the *Tek Sing's* storage spaces carefully and tightly.

This Chinese junk has a red hull. Is it from Canton or Amoy?

Deck a floor of the ship

Prow the front part of the ship, where a sailor watches for rocks and ships

Hull the outer covering of the junk

Anchor a heavy weight that holds the junk in one place

In 1822 Amoy was a busy seaport and one of the major centers in China for exporting tea.

First **porcelain** objects made of fine clay, such as cups, plates, bowls, spoons, and ornaments, were packed. These clay treasures came in various colors, from dark brown and orange to pale green and shiny white painted with beautiful blue flowers and swirls. Next boxes of tea, an important Chinese product, were loaded. Then came silk, bamboo furniture, writing paper, inks, glass beads, and other precious materials such as medicines.

Next bamboo canes, umbrellas, and other items that wouldn't be ruined by salt water were strapped to the outside of the junk. Every inch of space was filled! Merchants hoped to sell all of these goods in Java.

Finally about 2,000 people came aboard: 400 sailors and merchants and 1,600 other passengers, ranging in age from 6 to 70. Crowds of people standing on shore waved good-bye as the anchors were lifted. The sails were filled by a gentle breeze, and the junk slowly began moving south. The unlucky voyage had begun.

Workers in China today still make beautiful, hand-painted porcelain items.

3 On Board the *Tek Sing*

The deck on the *Tek Sing* was crowded because that was the only place for the passengers to live. For the next month, these people would cook rice on the deck and sleep on bamboo mats on the deck's wooden floor. The *Tek Sing* was only about 164 feet (50 meters) long and 33 feet (10 meters) wide. Therefore, these people had to live very closely together. Meanwhile merchants, the captain, and some of the sailors lived in straw-roofed cabins built on one end of the deck. The deck was a busy place both day and night because the junk had to sail 24 hours a day to complete the trip to Java in a month.

The emigrants on the *Tek Sing* slept on bamboo mats like these.

The sails in a junk contain sticks made of bamboo that keep the sails flat and make them strong.

Shortly after the voyage began, Io Tauko, the captain of the *Tek Sing*, made an important decision. Instead of following the regular route to Java, he chose a shortcut to the east and headed out to sea on a new route that would pass Gaspar Island.

No one knows why Io Tauko changed the course of the *Tek Sing*. Perhaps his junk had little drinking water left. Maybe it was too crowded for everyone to be comfortable for much longer. The captain might even have feared an attack by pirates. Whatever the reason, the *Tek Sing* ventured into waters where Chinese junks rarely sailed.

Because the *Tek Sing's* trip was such a long one, Captain Io Tauko might have changed his junk's course to try to reach Java faster.

Latitude and Longitude

Imaginary lines of latitude and longitude circle the globe and help people tell where they are. **Latitude** lines tell a sailor how far north or south a ship is. **Longitude** lines tell a sailor how far east or west a ship is. Lines of latitude are measured in degrees north or south of the equator. Latitudes north of the equator are marked °N, and latitudes to the south are marked °S. Lines of longitude are measured in degrees east or west of the Prime Meridian. Longitudes east of the Prime Meridian are marked °E and latitudes west of it are marked °W.

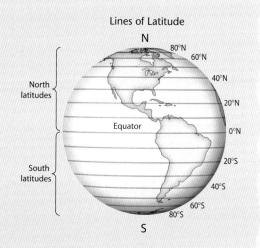

Lines of Latitude

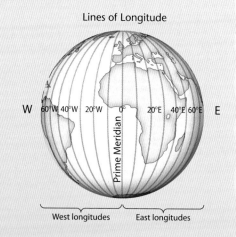

Lines of Longitude

The Route of the *Tek Sing*

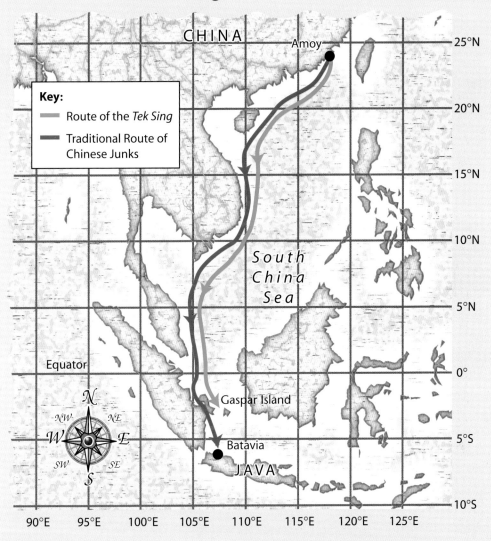

Amoy is near latitude line 25°N. To which line of
latitude is Batavia, Java, close?

Answer: Batavia is close to latitude line 5°S.

4 Sailing Across the South China Sea

The crew of the *Tek Sing* had many ways to sail their
ship through the waters of the South China Sea. During
the day, a sailor stood on the front of the ship to watch
for rocks and other boats. Sailors steered the junk
by observing the coastline of the land they were passing.
Because the early part of the journey was familiar to them,
they knew where to sail to avoid shallow waters and rocks.

The sailors of the *Tek Sing* often kept the coastline within sight so
that they would know their position, like this modern junk is doing.

From time to time, a sailor measured the depth of the sea. He would drop a rope with a lead weight on the end into the water until the weight hit the bottom. The length of the rope told how deep the water was. If the sea was too shallow, the ship might run into the bottom.

Measuring Water Depth

The weight on the end of the line was shaped like an upside-down bowl and smeared on the inside with sticky fat. Sand or mud from the ocean bottom stuck to the fat and told the crew what kind of ground they were sailing over.

By night the sailors used the stars to see which direction the ship was going. They looked at a star map with all of the known stars drawn on it. By comparing the stars in the night sky above them with the stars on their map, the sailors could tell where they were.

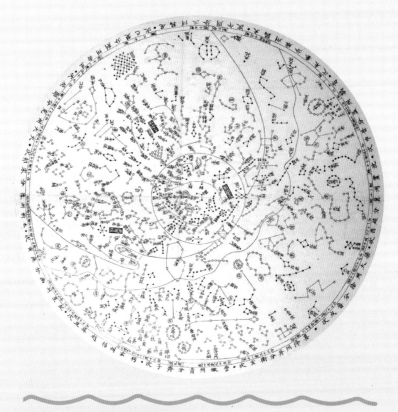

By charting and finding pictures in the stars, the Chinese people were able to tell where they were on Earth. This 1819 map shows the Chinese names for many stars.

The symbols on this 19th century Chinese compass label 24 directions.

However, during the day the sailors couldn't see the stars. Then they used a compass (a tool invented by the Chinese 700 years before) to guide their way. An iron needle that had been turned into a magnet floated in water inside the compass and pointed out directions.

The sailors of the *Tek Sing* had many tools to help guide them through the sea. However, as they began to take an unfamiliar route with night darkening the waters around them, they were missing one important thing: a **chart** of the area that could tell them where underwater rocks lay.

5 Rescue!

Soon after the *Tek Sing* had sunk, the *Indiana*, a small English trading ship, crossed the path of the doomed ship. Captain James Pearl of the *Indiana* had maps and charts to show him where dangerous rocks and shallow waters were.

Early on the morning of February 7, one of Captain Pearl's sailors reported a strange sight—many small rocks in the water that were not on the ship's sea chart. Then he noticed that the rocks were moving closer to the ship. Captain Pearl was called on deck, and instead of rocks, he saw boxes, umbrellas, and bamboo poles. Clinging to these floating objects were hundreds of Chinese people!

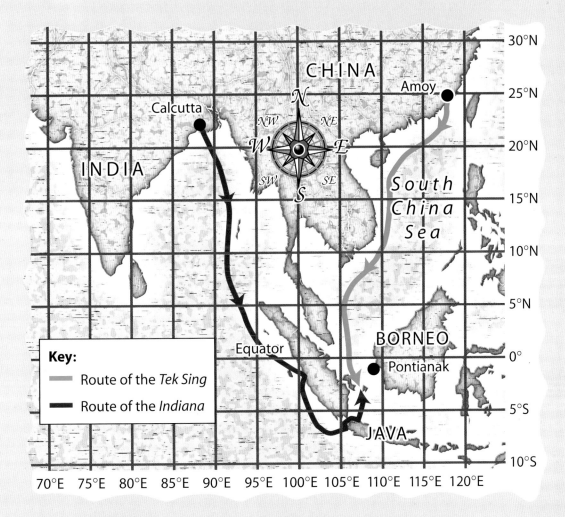

The *Indiana* was traveling from Calcutta, India, toward the island of Borneo. Calcutta is close to longitude line 90°E. To which line of longitude is Pontianak, Borneo, close?

Answer: Pontianak is close to longitude line 110°E.

Immediately Captain Pearl moved the *Indiana* toward the survivors and began lowering lifeboats to help bring them aboard. He warned his sailors to save people before goods. Over the next few hours, Captain Pearl and his crew worked through heavy rains and strong winds to rescue as many people as they could. Some people were pulled directly from the sea. Others were saved from tiny Gaspar Island, where they had been thrown by the fierce waters.

The rescue finished, Captain Pearl climbed to the highest part of Gaspar Island. Looking at the sea through a telescope, he saw nothing left of the *Tek Sing*.

Of the 2,000 people who were thrown from the *Tek Sing*, Captain Pearl saved the lives of 190. One hundred eighty were people whom he took with him to Borneo, where he left them. Ten were traders and shopkeepers who stayed on board the *Indiana* with Captain Pearl and his crew. All of these people were probably disappointed not to meet their family and friends in Java . . . but at least they were alive.

6 An Important Discovery

Over 150 years later, in May of 1999, the *Restless M*, an 82-foot (25 meters) ship, sailed the waters near Gaspar Island looking for shipwrecks. For almost 30 years, teams of scientists had been searching the South China Sea for sunken treasure and ships to study. Sometimes they used old maps of an ancient water route Chinese trade ships traveled to reach other countries to tell them where ships were most likely to have sunk.

The *Restless M* searched the waters of the South China Sea for sunken treasure.

The crew of the *Restless M* dived near the Belvidere Shoals.

However, the crew of the *Restless M* had more exact information. They had read in a 100-year-old book about a large junk that had sunk near the southwest tip of the Belvidere **Shoals,** a group of large underwater rocks and coral **reefs** close to Gaspar Island. The book told them that this southwest tip was located at latitude 2°S. Therefore, they focused their search on this area.

Unfortunately, the crew had been searching for weeks, but found nothing. Each day of the search cost more than 10,000 dollars, and money was running out. In two days, they would have to give up and go home.

Suddenly a mound appeared on the screen of one of the instruments the crew was using to look at the sea floor. Two divers traveled 96 feet (30 meters) below the surface to see what the mound was. They discovered three large, iron rings: the metal bands that had once supported three huge masts. They had found a junk—a large one!

Michael Hatcher, who had found several important shipwrecks before, dived down to see it for himself. He spotted cups, plates, bowls, pots, vases, and small statues—huge quantities of porcelain in piles all over the ocean floor.

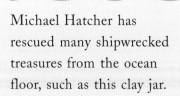

Michael Hatcher has rescued many shipwrecked treasures from the ocean floor, such as this clay jar.

Michael knew his crew had made a big discovery when he saw all of these porcelain items spread over the sea floor. Porcelain is so valuable that some people call it white gold!

Michael called an expert on shipwrecks, Nigel Pickford. Nigel made a note of the latitude and longitude where the wreck was found. Then he began searching historical records to find a junk that might have sunk in that position. In an old newspaper, he found a story about Captain Pearl and the Chinese people whom Captain Pearl and his crew had saved near Gaspar Island. The crew of the *Restless M* had found the *Tek Sing!*

7 *Tek Sing* Treasures

Michael Hatcher hired a special boat to begin gathering items from the wreck, and the divers started working. They found glass bottles, stone lion statues, pocket watches, metal cannons, hairpins, candlesticks, and coins scattered all around the wreck. However, the Chinese porcelain they found was their most exciting discovery. There were more than 350,000 pieces of it—the largest amount of porcelain ever rescued from the sea!

All together Michael and the other divers spent 2,250 hours bringing *Tek Sing* treasures to the surface.

The *Tek Sing* was carrying different types of porcelain, and some pieces are over 500 years old. Artists could study these pieces of porcelain and find out when each kind of porcelain was created and how it was made. They are learning a lot about Chinese art from the contents of the *Tek Sing*.

Looking closely at porcelain from the *Tek Sing* can tell us things about how Chinese people lived in the past.

Orange and white patches of coral had begun to grow on some of the porcelain pieces. Others were just a little sandy and could be rinsed off by hand. Many were still packed the same way they'd been when the junk sank.

These porcelain dishes from the *Tek Sing* were found still in tidy stacks.

Some of the porcelain items from the *Tek Sing* had coral growing on them.

Workers sorted through the porcelain dishes after they were brought to the surface.

There were tiny blue and white teacups and bright red teapots. There were brown teapots with dragons on the sides and big, clay stoves. There were enough blue and white bowls, plates, and cups to serve hundreds of people. Blue blossoms, butterflies, people, and animals are painted on the sides of much of the porcelain in great detail.

The discovery of the *Tek Sing* helps us better understand Chinese history. Some of the treasures found in it were goods to sell, while others belonged to its passengers. However, all of these treasures can tell us about past Chinese life. We can study the items found on board and discover what goods the Chinese people traded with other places. We can also learn what was valued by Chinese people back then.

Tiny sculptures and painted spoons were used and valued by the passengers of the *Tek Sing*.

After the porcelain objects of the *Tek Sing* were cleaned, they were sold to new owners. Now many people today can enjoy the beautiful treasures once lost with this ship.

For many years, the *Tek Sing* was hidden beneath the waves of the South China Sea, forgotten. However, now it will be remembered for many years to come. The items saved from the *Tek Sing* can help us imagine life aboard this junk and recall with respect the last journey that its passengers took.

Glossary

chart a map that shows sailors where coasts and shallow ground are

emigrate to leave your country and go live in another

junk a type of Chinese boat

latitude imaginary lines measured in degrees that tell how far north or south something is

longitude imaginary lines measured in degrees that tell how far east or west something is

porcelain objects made from special clay

reef a group of rocks or coral either underwater or just above the surface

shoal shallow water in the sea

Index